CRAFT ★ STAR

Green Crafts

Editor: Rebecca J. Razo
Assistant Editor: Stephanie Fitzgerald
Art Direction: Shelley Baugh
Production Design: Debbie Aiken
Production Management: Irene Chan, Lawrence Marquez,
and Nicole Szawlowski
Crafter: Megan Friday
Writers: Rebecca J. Razo and Stephanie Fitzgerald
Illustrator: Diana Fisher
Photographer: Joel Schnell
Copyeditor: Jickie Torres

Walter Foster Publishing, Inc.
3 Wrigley, Suite A
Irvine, CA 92618
www.walterfoster.com

Printed in China.

3 5 7 9 10 8 6 4 2

Green Crafts

Become an Earth-Friendly Craft Star, Step by Easy Step!

By Megan Friday

Table of Contents

Meet Megan 6

Let's Get Green! 7

Tools & Materials 8

"Go Green" Tote Bag 10

Fabric Tree Tote Bag 14

On-the-Go Water Bottles 18

Big News Picture Frame 22

"Live Green" T-shirt 24

Fabric Squares Reusable Gift Bag 28

Leaf Stamps Reusable Gift Bag 32

Hand-painted Reusable Gift Bag 36

Earth Day Cookie Jar & Recipe 38

Bright Idea Lightswitch Plate 40

Recycled Glass Fancy Vases 44

Magnificent Magnets 46

Three R's Flowerpots 48

Ms. Green Jeans 52

Map Your Way Stationery Kit 54

Decorative Decoupage 58

Project Templates 62

Get Involved! 64

Meet Megan

A self-taught crafter, Megan Friday enjoys doing anything creative—including knitting, sewing, crafting, cooking, and photography. Megan was an early childhood educator for 12 years before taking time to raise her son and daughter. She currently juggles freelance crafting with her many responsibilities as a doting mom, devoted pet owner, and environmentally aware consumer. When she has a free moment to spare, Megan enjoys hiking, traveling, reading, and studying child development. Her creative inspiration comes from her family and friends, animals, nature, and beautiful fabrics and prints. Megan is married to a graphic designer and lives with her family in Boulder, Colorado.

Let's Get Green!

Do you enjoy making crafts and taking care of the planet? Well here's your chance to do both! With this helpful book as your guide, you will never look at discarded cans, newspapers, and cereal boxes in the same way again. Transform glass baby-food jars into fanciful decorative vases and then use the lids to make quirky refrigerator magnets; give your worn-out plastic water bottle a lift with the help of some ribbon and glue; turn an old glass bowl into a decoupaged work of art; or jazz up a plain T-shirt with an earth-friendly message. The projects in this book will have your creativity soaring in no time—and earn you a little thank you from Mother Nature, too! Being green and crafty has never been so much fun!

Tools & Materials

Here are some of the supplies you'll need to complete the projects in this book. Keep in mind that each craft has its own materials list too, and some items may not be shown in this section. To get started, gather the following basic tools: scissors, pencil, pen, and a black felt-tip permanent marker. Then look over this page and review the materials listed for each project to see what else you'll need.

hole punch

sponge

masking tape

paper towels

craft glue

drawing pencil

black felt-tip permanent marker

paintbrush

foam brush

craft knife

paints

scissors

"Go Green" Tote Bag

Say goodbye to plastic bags forever. Display your green pride with this handy substitute!

It takes up to a thousand years for plastic bags to break down.

Materials

- Canvas tote bag
- Dimensional or "puffy" fabric paint in squeezable bottle
- Regular fabric paint (2 shades of green; brown)
- Kitchen sponge
- Scissors
- Pencil
- Small paintbrush
- Paper towels

Use a pencil to draw a branch outline on the tote. Then trace over the outline using dimensional fabric paint, and allow the paint to dry overnight.

Using regular fabric paint and a small paintbrush, fill in the branch.

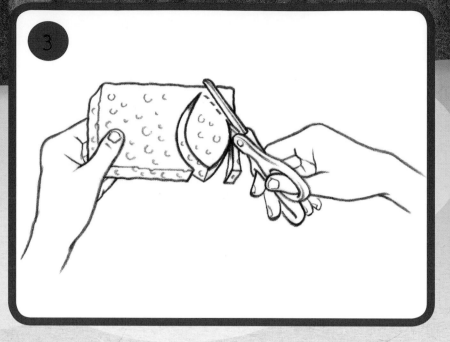

3

Cut out a leaf shape from a kitchen sponge.

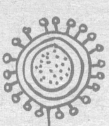

Lightly dip the flat surface of the sponge in one color of fabric paint; blot once on a paper towel and then stamp leaves along the branch. Rinse sponge and repeat using your other color.

4

5

Use a pencil to draw block letters on the tote with an environmental slogan. Trace the lines with dimensional fabric paint; allow paint to dry overnight.

6

Using regular fabric paint and a small paintbrush, fill in the letters.

Fabric Tree Tote Bag

Earth-friendly tote bags are handy, durable, and reusable.

Materials

- Canvas tote bag
- Dimensional or "puffy" fabric paint in squeezable bottle
- Regular fabric paint (light green)
- Fabric scrap for treetop
- Contrasting fabric scrap for tree trunk
- All-purpose waterproof sealer
- Scissors
- Pencil
- Small paintbrush
- Tree trunk template on page 62

Use a large kitchen bowl to trace a circle on the underside of the treetop fabric; then cut out the pattern.

Place the treetop fabric in the desired position on the tote and trim off any extra material. Cover the back of the fabric with sealer and then secure it to the tote. Smooth out any wrinkles or bubbles.

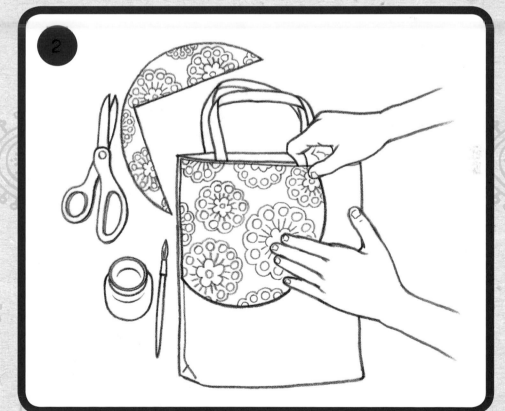

Use the template on page 62 as a guide to draw the tree trunk onto the back of the second fabric; then cut out the pattern.

Secure the tree trunk fabric to the tote in the desired position following the directions in step 2. Brush a coat of sealer over the entire surface of the tree, covering both fabrics. Allow to dry.

Use a pencil to draw block letters on the tote with your favorite environmental slogan. Trace the lines of your letters with dimensional fabric paint, and allow the paint to dry overnight.

Using regular fabric paint and a small paintbrush, fill in the letters.

On-the-Go Water Bottles

Turn an old water bottle from drab to fab in minutes, and your H_2O will taste better than ever!

Materials

- Plastic water bottle
- Assorted ribbon about 3–5 yards in length
- All-purpose waterproof sealer
- Foam brush
- Scissors

1

Use the foam brush to cover the entire water bottle with a thin coat of sealer. Allow to dry.

Wrap one ribbon around the circumference of the water bottle and add 2″; then cut. Cut the remaining ribbons to this length. You will need about 8 to 12 ribbon strips.

2

Starting at the bottom of the bottle, apply a fresh coat of sealer and then secure a strip of ribbon around the bottle. Trim the ribbon so there is only a small amount of overlap.

Line up the edge of the next ribbon with the one below it so that the start of each new ribbon strip lines up from the bottom to the top; repeat step 3.

5

Continue this process up the bottle placing each ribbon strip directly above the one beneath it, without overlapping or leaving any gaps.

6

Finish by coating the entire bottle with several layers of sealer, making sure to cover the entire surface. Allow for proper drying times between coats.

Big News Picture Frame

Extra! Extra! Display your favorite photo in a frame with eco-friendly messages that are sure to make headlines.

Materials

- Picture frame with a wide, flat surface
- Newspaper
- Magazines
- All-purpose waterproof sealer
- Foam brush
- Scissors

More than 200 million trees would be saved each year if every newspaper were recycled!

1

2

3

Cut out four newspaper strips, each large enough to cover the entire surface of the frame. Use sealer to glue each strip of newspaper to the frame.

Cover the surface of the frame with a layer of sealer to coat. Smooth out any wrinkles or bubbles. Allow it to dry completely.

Search through magazines to clip out environmental slogans, expressions, and images, or cut out individual letters to spell earth-friendly messages.

4

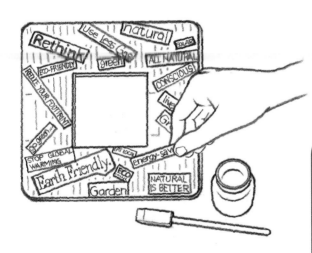

Place the cutouts around the frame in the desired position before gluing them down. When they are placed where you want them, use the sealer to adhere them over the newspaper.

5

Apply several coats of sealer over the entire surface of the frame to seal. Allow for proper drying times between coats.

"Live Green" T-shirt

Everyone looks better in green! Embellish a plain T-shirt to help spread the word!

24

1

To make the stencil, write the words "Live Green" in large block letters across the paperboard, sizing them to fit the T-shirt. Carefully cut out the letters.

T-shirt

Place another large piece of paperboard inside the T-shirt to prevent the paint from bleeding through; lay the T-shirt on a flat surface and smooth out the wrinkles. Place the stencil on the center of the shirt and secure it on all four sides with the tape.

2

LIVE GREEN

3

Dip the small sponge in the fabric paint and blot once on a paper towel. Dab the sponge lightly over the surface of the stencil completely filling in all of the letters. Carefully remove the tape and lift the stencil from the shirt. Allow the paint to dry completely.

Using the letters on the T-shirt as a guide, draw a large, curved arrow on paperboard; then cut it out to make a second stencil.

4

5

Using the new stencil, repeat the process described in steps 2 and 3 to create a circle of arrows around the slogan. Allow the paint to dry. Use fabric glue to apply embellishments, if desired.

Did you know that old shoe boxes can be recycled into new cereal boxes and pizza cartons?

Craft Tip

For some letter stencils, you may need to leave a gap between lines, as shown in this R. This will make cutting them out a breeze, and your letters will be perfect every time!

Fabric Squares Reusable Gift Bag

Save a tree (or two or three!) with snazzy gift bags that keep on giving.

Materials

- Paper gift bag, handles removed
- Fabric scraps cut into 2"–3" squares or rectangles
- All-purpose waterproof sealer
- Foam brush
- Scissors
- Paperboard from a cereal box
- Clothespin (optional)

fabric squares

clothespins

Lay bag flat on one side. Spread a thin layer of sealer over the entire front surface with the foam brush.

Place the fabric squares on the bag one by one, covering the entire surface. You may need to trim some of the squares so that they fit side by side without overlapping. Smooth them flat.

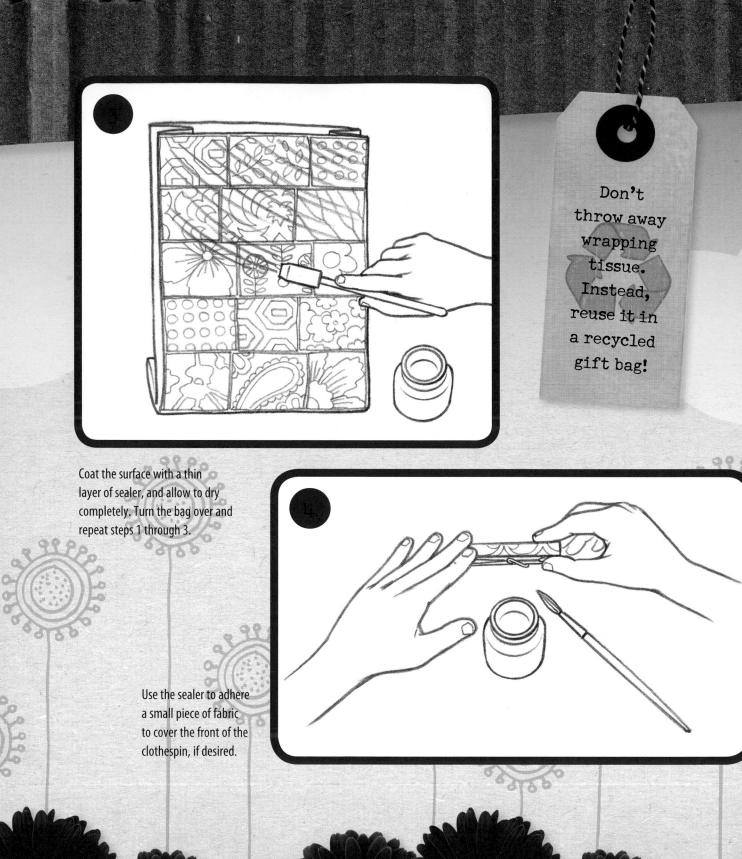

Don't throw away wrapping tissue. Instead, reuse it in a recycled gift bag!

Coat the surface with a thin layer of sealer, and allow to dry completely. Turn the bag over and repeat steps 1 through 3.

Use the sealer to adhere a small piece of fabric to cover the front of the clothespin, if desired.

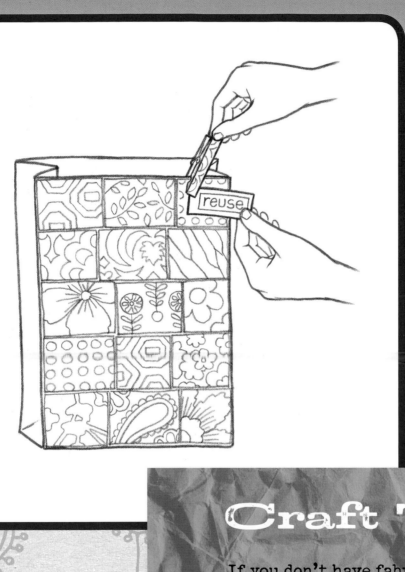

Make a tag using recycled paperboard, and use the clothespin to attach it to the bag.

Craft Tip

If you don't have fabric scraps, cut up an old T-shirt or blouse that has a bright, funky pattern. (But first make sure to ask your mom or dad if it's ok!)

Leaf Stamps Reusable Gift Bag

This BAG was Handcrafted for REUSE!

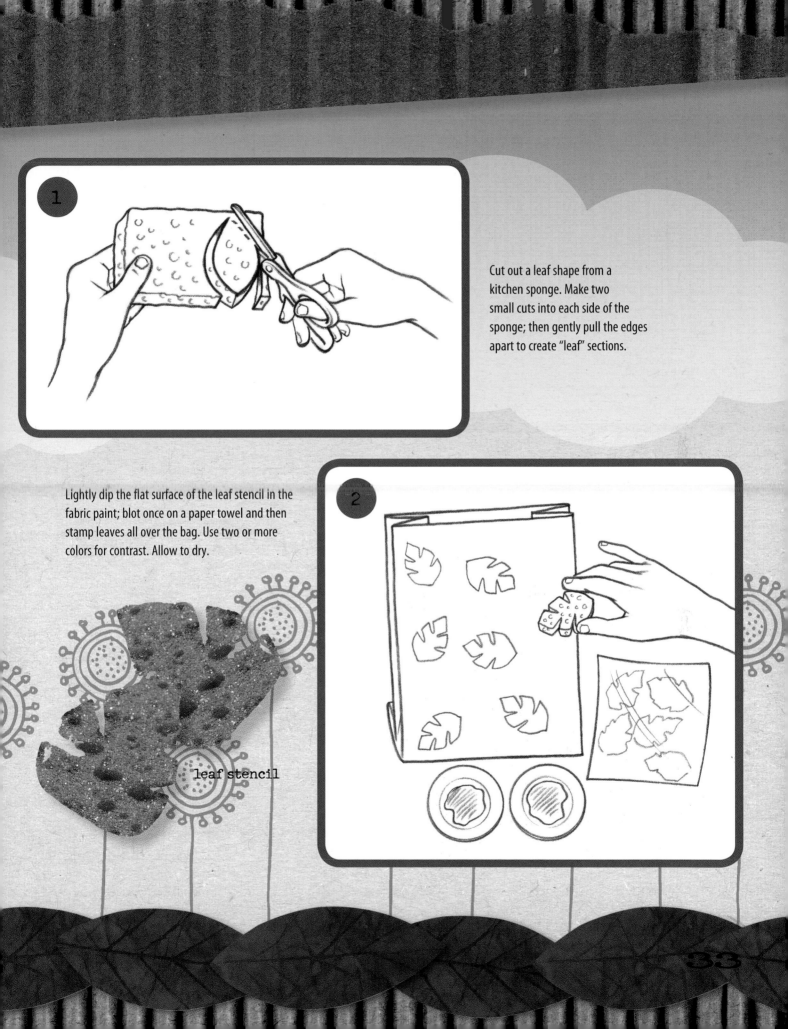

1

Cut out a leaf shape from a kitchen sponge. Make two small cuts into each side of the sponge; then gently pull the edges apart to create "leaf" sections.

Lightly dip the flat surface of the leaf stencil in the fabric paint; blot once on a paper towel and then stamp leaves all over the bag. Use two or more colors for contrast. Allow to dry.

leaf stencil

2

3

Dip the small paintbrush in brown paint. Blot lightly on a paper towel and then paint a stem on each leaf.

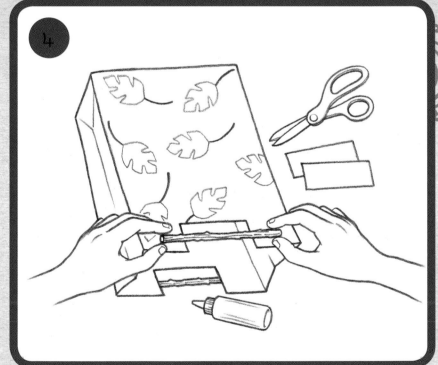

4

Handles: Lay the bag flat and cut 3-1/4" x 1-1/4" rectangles out of the top of both sides of the bag. Position one twig across the top of each side of the bag, and glue the ends in place.

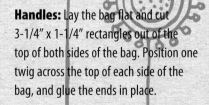

Punch four holes through *each* side of the bag: one above and one below each end of the twig. String twine through each pair of holes and pull to fasten around the ends of the twigs to secure them in place. Knot the twine on the inside of the bag tightly; then cut the loose ends.

twine

Craft Tip

Make a hangtag from the paperboard of a cereal box. Loop twine through a hole punched at the top and affix to the bag. Write a message encouraging reuse.

East or West, Green is best!

Hand-painted Reusable Gift Bag

Materials

- Paper gift bag, handles removed
- Acrylic or tempera paints (2 or more colors)
- Small paintbrushes
- Hole punch
- Pipe cleaner in matching colors
- Paperboard from a cereal box

PLEASE REUSE THIS BAG!

gift bag

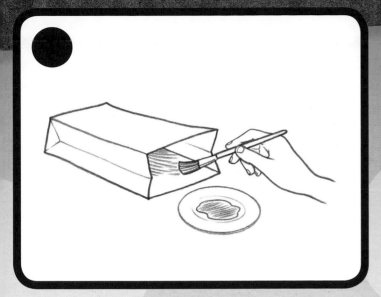

Paint the inside of the bag one color; allow to dry.

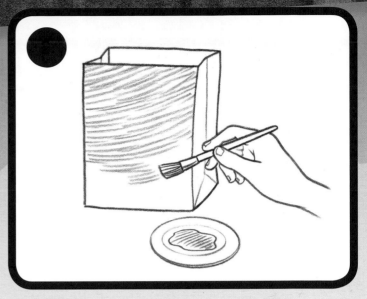

Paint the exterior of the bag a contrasting color (you may need two coats of paint); allow to dry completely between coats.

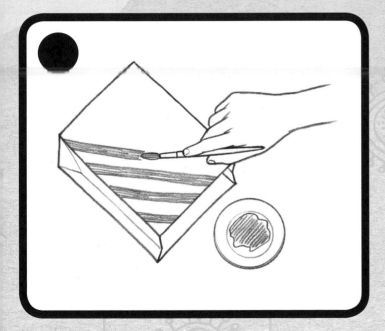

Use a contrasting color to paint patterns on the bag.

Punch two holes through each side of the top of the bag about 4"–6" apart, depending on the size of the bag. Loop pipe cleaner through the holes to make handles and glue in place. Write an environmentally friendly message directly on the bag, or make a hangtag out of paperboard (see the Craft Tip on page 35).

Earth Day Cookie Jar & Recipe

Celebrate Earth Day as it was meant to be celebrated: with green-swirl cookies!

Materials

- Earth Day Cookies
- Recycled glass jar with lid
- Paperboard from a cereal box, cut into a rectangle
- Twine, ribbon, or string
- Hole punch

Earth Day is April 22.

Celebrate earth day everyday cookies!!

Steps

1. Make cookies according to the recipe.
2. Package cookies in a recycled glass jar.
3. Hole punch the end of the paperboard, and write a message encouraging friends to celebrate Earth Day.
4. Loop a piece of ribbon or twine through the card and wrap it around the top of the jar beneath the lid.

Earth Day Cookies

INGREDIENTS

1 cup butter, softened to room temperature
1 cup light brown sugar, packed
1 egg, room temperature
2 teaspoons vanilla

1/2 teaspoon baking soda
1/2 teaspoon salt
2 cups all purpose flour
Green and blue food coloring

DIRECTIONS

1. In a large bowl, beat the butter and brown sugar using an electric mixer until light and fluffy.
2. Add the egg and vanilla; beat until well mixed.
3. Add the baking soda and salt; mix to combine. Slowly add the flour and beat until just combined.
4. Divide the dough into two equal portions. Add several drops of blue food coloring to one portion and several drops of green food coloring to the other.
5. Flatten each colored section of dough into a rectangular shape; chill for 1 to 2 hours.
6. Spread flour on a work surface, and use a rolling pin to roll out each portion separately, creating 1/4"-thick rectangles measuring approximately 12" x 8 ".
7. Place the green rectangle on top of the blue rectangle with the long edge facing you.
8. With a knife, slice the double-layered rectangle vertically into two smaller rectangles measuring approximately 6" x 8" long.
9. Use your hands to roll each of the smaller rectangles into long, tight tubes starting with the long edge. Roll the tube back and forth on a flat surface to smooth out the overlap.
10. Wrap tubes in plastic wrap and chill overnight.

To Bake:

1. Heat oven to 350 degrees.
2. Remove plastic wrap from dough. Slice each tube into several 1/4"-thick slices. Place the slices on an ungreased baking sheet, leaving about 1/2" between cookies.
3. Bake for 9–12 minutes. Allow to cool briefly on the cookie sheet; then remove to cool on a flat surface.

Bright Idea Lightswitch Plate

Illuminate the importance of energy conservation with a lightswitch plate reminder.

Materials

- Plain lightswitch plate
- Decorative paper or newspaper
- Magazines
- All-purpose waterproof sealer
- Scissors
- Craft knife
- Foam brush
- Pencil

decorative paper

Place the lightswitch plate upside down on the decorative paper or newspaper. Trace around the plate; then cut out the paper.

Coat front of plate with sealer and carefully apply the paper, lining up the sides and smoothing the surface. Don't worry about covering the openings; you'll cut those out later.

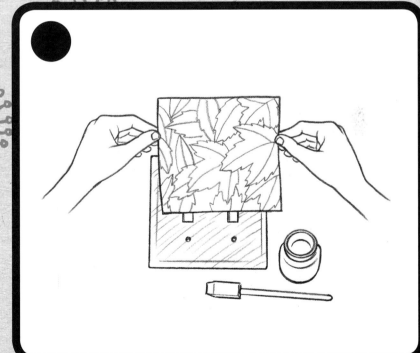

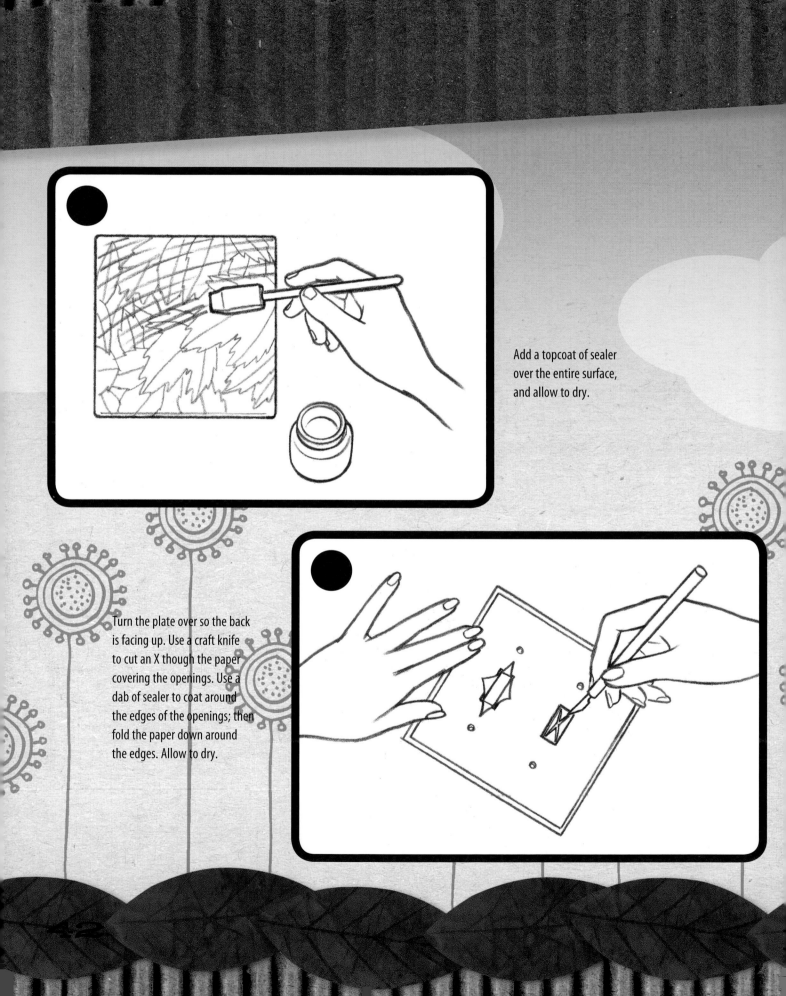

Add a topcoat of sealer over the entire surface, and allow to dry.

Turn the plate over so the back is facing up. Use a craft knife to cut an X though the paper covering the openings. Use a dab of sealer to coat around the edges of the openings; then fold the paper down around the edges. Allow to dry.

Cut out letters from magazines to spell out energy-conservation messages. Arrange the letters on the plate in the desired position; then use the sealer to apply them. Cover the entire surface with two more layers of sealer, allowing for proper drying times between each coat.

Safety Tip

Ask for an adult's help before using the craft knife.

Recycled Glass Fancy Vases

Brighten your days with colorful recycled glass decorative vases.

Materials

- Clean baby food jars (save the lids for the Magnificent Magnets project on page 46)
- Colored tissue paper
- All-purpose waterproof sealer
- Foam brush
- Fine-gauge wire
- Scissors
- Craft-wire cutters
- Large paper craft punches in assorted designs (optional)

Use scissors to cut out several shapes from the tissue paper, or use a combination of craft punches for some shapes and scissors for others. Use the jar as a guide to determine the sizes.

Use the foam brush to coat the outside of the entire jar with a layer of sealer. Carefully apply the tissue shapes on the jar in the desired locations; smooth out any wrinkles and bubbles. Add three more layers of sealer to the outside of the jar, allowing proper drying times between each coat.

Cut two pieces of wire, each approximately 4' long, and fold them in half, as shown. Wrap one of the wires around the circumference of the jar under the lip, as if you are going to make a bow. Cross the ends and wrap them back around to the other side.

Twist the pieces together tightly until the wire is securely fastened around the lip of the jar and you have formed one side of the hanger. Repeat step 3 using the second piece of folded wire, starting on the opposite side of the jar.

Continue twisting each end of wire together tightly while simultaneously bringing them up to meet each other. Now, twist both ends together to form the complete hanger.

Craft Tip

Use your pretty vases outside as tealight candle holders, or use them indoors to display fresh flowers, colorful beads, or sand art.

Magnificent Magnets

Go ahead, flip a lid and get crazy crafting some awesome magnets for the fridge.

Materials

- Lids from baby food jars and/or large bottle caps
- Photos and/or paper cutouts
- All-purpose waterproof sealer
- Craft glue
- Scissors
- Pencil
- Small round or square magnets (available in craft stores)

Gather photos of friends, family, pets, or special places that can be cut to fit inside the lids and bottle caps.

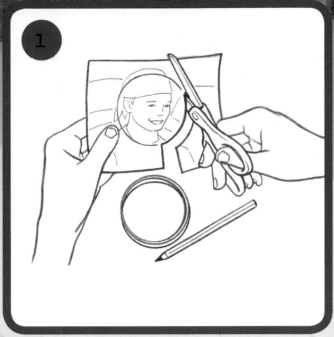

Position the lid or bottle cap around the desired scene in a photo. Use a pencil to trace around the lid; then cut the scene from the photo.

Use craft glue to secure the photo inside the lid; then coat with several layers of sealer, allowing for proper drying times between each coat.

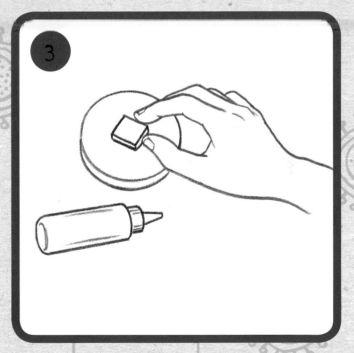

Use craft glue to secure a magnet to the top of the lid or bottle cap. Allow to dry overnight.

47

Three R's Flowerpots

Use your flower power to create a new home for some sweet smelling blooming beauties!

Materials

- Three large aluminum cans (28-ounce cans work best)
- Acrylic paint
- Paintbrushes
- Ribbon
- Craft glue
- Craft sticks
- Paperboard from a cereal box

Safety Tip

Before working with empty cans, have an adult check for sharp edges.

craft sticks

ribbon

seedling

RECYCLE!

Wash cans thoroughly with warm, soapy water. Paint each can with several coats of acrylic paint. Allow cans to dry thoroughly between coats.

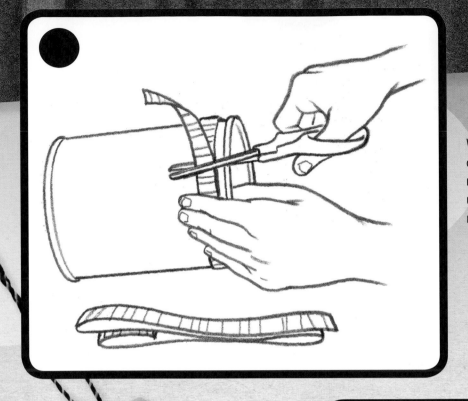

Wrap one ribbon around the circumference of one can. Cut the ribbon in the appropriate spot; then use it to measure out the length of the remaining ribbon strips.

Studies show that exposure to plants and flowers improves mood and decreases stress!

Use craft glue to apply one ribbon around the top of the can and one ribbon around the bottom.

Cut a piece of paperboard into a small rectangle. Glue one end of the craft stick to the back to create a sign. Cut two small strips of matching ribbon and glue them to each side of the paperboard.

Plant each can with indoor flowers, or fill with rice or sand to support artificial flowers.

Ms. Green Jeans

Hey, Green Jeans! Now you can tote your cell phone everywhere in totally green style! It's sew easy!

Materials

- One pair of used jeans with fold-over flaps on the rear pockets
- Fabric scissors
- Fabric or craft glue
- Dimensional or "puffy" fabric paint in squeezable bottle (optional)
- Colored buttons, rhinestones, or other embellishments (optional)

jeans

Use fabric scissors to cut into the jeans around one rear pocket leaving a 1/8"–1/4" border so the pocket remains intact.

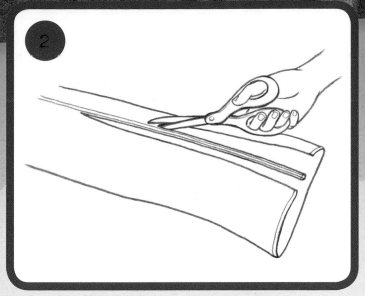

Cut down the length of one jean leg on each side of the thick inner seam so that you'll have one long strip of strong denim, approximately 1/2"–3/4" wide. Determine how long you want the strap to be. For a shoulder bag, you may want to keep the length as is. For a handbag, 16"–20" long is appropriate.

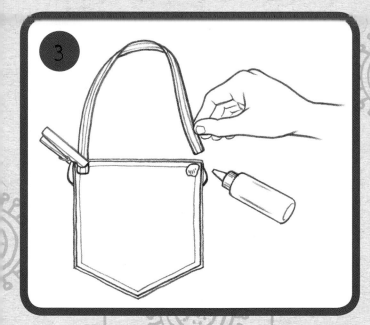

Using a generous amount of fabric glue, attach each end of the strap to the top back corners of the pocket. Allow to dry for 24 to 48 hours. Secure the pieces with clothespins if possible to help seal the bond.

Add any embellishments such as buttons or rhinestones, and/or "write" your initials with puffy fabric paint.

Map Your Way Stationery Kit

Recycled maps will help guide the way as you create nifty notecards, postcards, and envelopes.

AIR MAIL

TO:

Materials

- Recycled maps
- Envelope template on page 63
- All-purpose waterproof sealer
- Tracing paper or vellum
- Paperboard from a cereal box
- Hole punch
- Glue stick
- Scissors
- Waterproof marker
- Twine
- Pencil

1

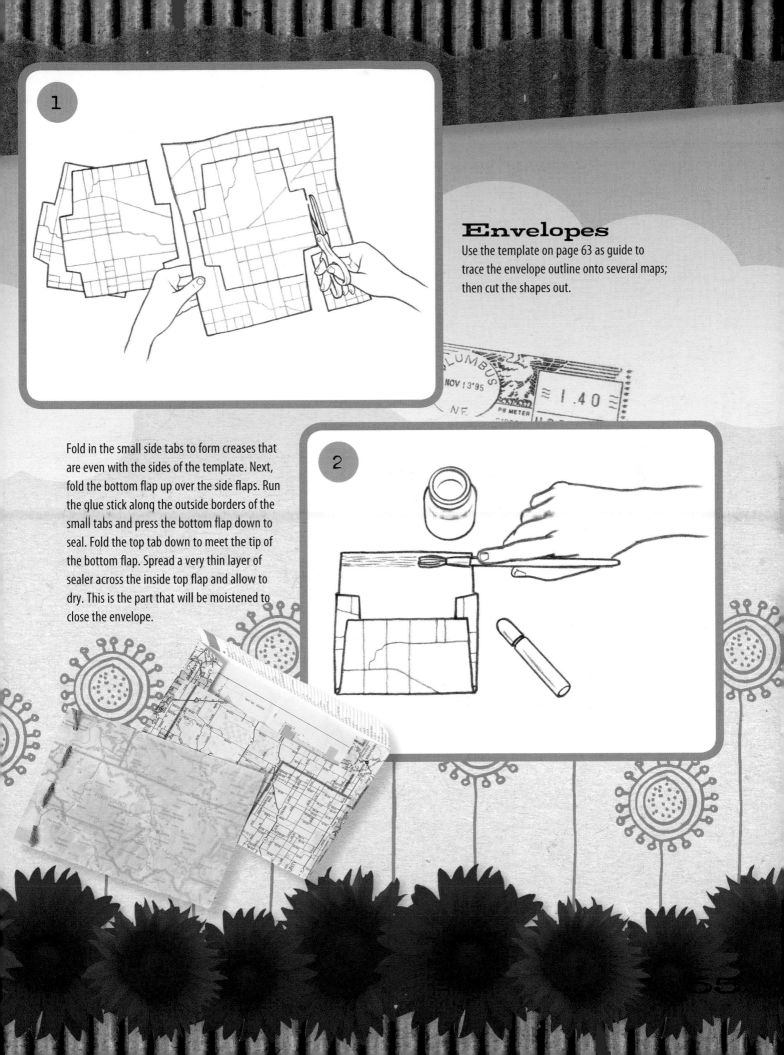

Envelopes

Use the template on page 63 as guide to trace the envelope outline onto several maps; then cut the shapes out.

Fold in the small side tabs to form creases that are even with the sides of the template. Next, fold the bottom flap up over the side flaps. Run the glue stick along the outside borders of the small tabs and press the bottom flap down to seal. Fold the top tab down to meet the tip of the bottom flap. Spread a very thin layer of sealer across the inside top flap and allow to dry. This is the part that will be moistened to close the envelope.

2

Notecards

Cut pieces of map and tracing paper into 3-1/2" x 5" rectangles; then layer the tracing paper over the map paper.

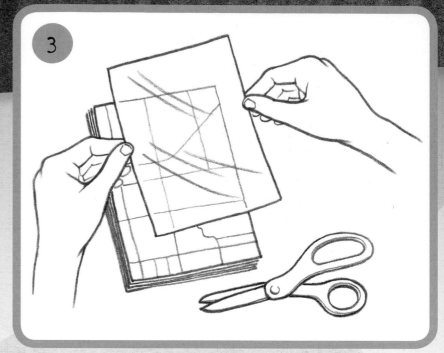

3

4

Punch 6 holes across one short end of the rectangle through both the map and tracing paper, as close to the edge as possible. Cut the twine approximately 3-1/2" long and weave it through the holes starting and ending on top of the tracing paper. Knot the twine on both ends.

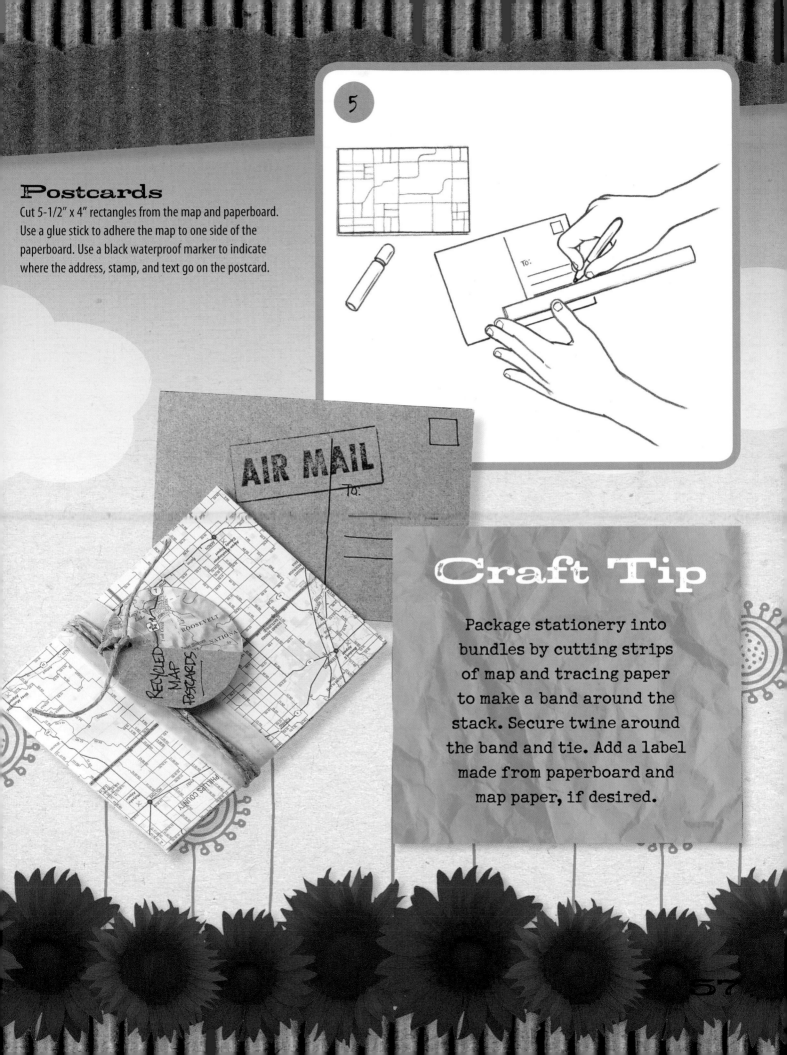

Postcards

Cut 5-1/2" x 4" rectangles from the map and paperboard. Use a glue stick to adhere the map to one side of the paperboard. Use a black waterproof marker to indicate where the address, stamp, and text go on the postcard.

5

AIR MAIL

To:

RECYCLED MAP POSTCARDS

Craft Tip

Package stationery into bundles by cutting strips of map and tracing paper to make a band around the stack. Secure twine around the band and tie. Add a label made from paperboard and map paper, if desired.

Decorative Decoupage

Transform an ordinary glass bowl into an extraordinary work of art!

Materials

- Clear glass bowl
- Colorful tissue, origami, or construction paper
- All-purpose waterproof sealer
- Foam brush
- Scissors
- Acrylic paint

Glass never wears out! It can be reused and recycled forever.

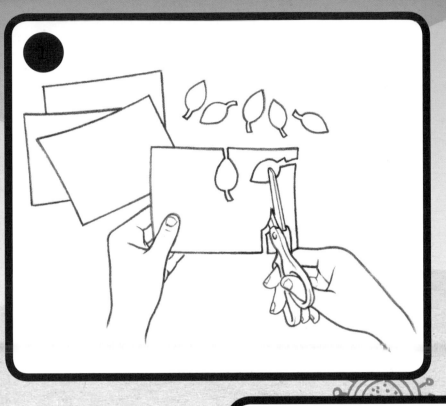

clear glass bowl

Cut several leaf shapes from multi-colored paper. Use the bowl as a guide to determine shapes, sizes, and quantity.

Turn your bowl upside down and use the foam brush to cover the entire outside surface with a thin coat of sealer.

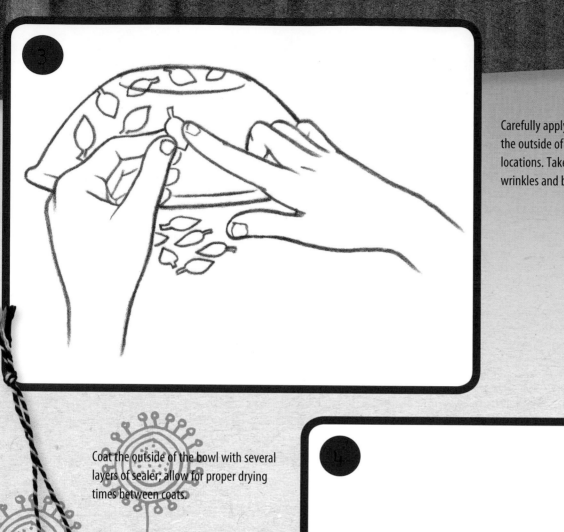

3

Carefully apply the paper leaves around the outside of the bowl in the desired locations. Take care to smooth out wrinkles and bubbles.

Coat the outside of the bowl with several layers of sealer; allow for proper drying times between coats.

4

Did you know that it can take as many as 1 million years for glass bottles to decompose?

Once the bowl is dry, use the foam brush to paint over the decoupaged leaves, covering them completely. You will need to coat the bowl with several layers of paint to ensure a good opaque paint finish. Allow for proper drying times between coats. Once the final coat of paint is dry, brush on several more coats of sealer, allowing for proper drying times between each.

Craft Tip

Decoupaged bowls aren't dishwasher safe. Handwash your bowl using lukewarm water, mild soap, and a soft cloth.

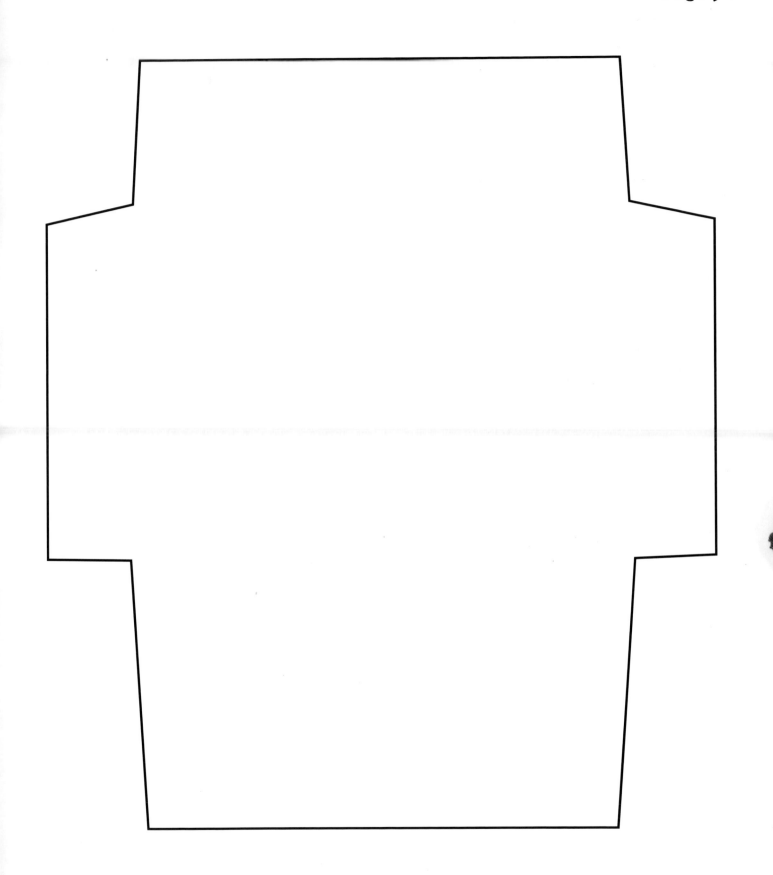

Get Involved!

There are many things you can do locally to reduce your carbon footprint globally and live a little greener:

- Volunteer with an environmental organization
- Plant trees and flowers
- Clean up beaches, parks, and fields in your community
- Use energy-efficient light bulbs at home
- Recycle! Plastic, paper, aluminum, glass, steel, cardboard, metal cans, printer cartridges, batteries, computers, and other electronic equipment can all be recycled. Check with your local municipality to find recycling drop-off locations in your area
- Walk, ride your bike, or use public transportation whenever possible
- And always remember to...

reduce Reuse recycle